Crabapples

BUGS
and other insects

Bobbie Kalman & Tammy Everts
🌳 Crabtree Publishing Company

Crabapples

created by Bobbie Kalman

for Selina Appleby

Editor-in-Chief
Bobbie Kalman

Writing team
Bobbie Kalman
Tammy Everts

Managing editor
Lynda Hale

Editors
Petrina Gentile
David Schimpky
Janine Schaub

Computer design
Lynda Hale
David Schimpky

Separations and film
Dot 'n Line Image Inc.

Printer
Worzalla Publishing Company

Illustrations
Antoinette "Cookie" DeBiasi: pages 17, 22-23
Tammy Everts: pages 5, 6, 10, 11, 14-15, 25

Photographs
J. Alcock/Visuals Unlimited: page 19 (left)
Bill Beatty/Visuals Unlimited: page 8
John D. Cunningham/Visuals Unlimited: pages 12, 29 (top)
John Daly: page 7 (bottom left)
Patrick H. Davies: pages 26, 30 (top)
David M. Dennis/Tom Stack & Associates: pages 9 (bottom), 13 (right), 17, 20 (top)
Don W. Fawcett/Visuals Unlimited: page 19 (right)
Kerry T. Givens/Tom Stack & Associates: pages 5, 9 (center)
Bill Johnson/Visuals Unlimited: page 25
Diane Payton Majumdar: pages 7 (top right, bottom right), 10, 13 (left), 21 (both), 23 (bottom), 29 (bottom), 30 (bottom)
Jane McAlonan/Visuals Unlimited: page 20 (bottom)
John A. McDonald: pages 7 (top left), 23 (top)
Glen M. Oliver/Visuals Unlimited: page 30 (center)
Don and Esther Phillips/Tom Stack & Associates: title page
Rod Planck/Tom Stack & Associates: pages 4, 9 (top), 24
D. A. Rinfoul/Visuals Unlimited: page 27
Kjell B. Sandved/Visuals Unlimited: cover, pages 16, 18
Kevin Schaffer/Visuals Unlimited: page 28
Y. Robert Tymstra: page 11

Crabtree Publishing Company

350 Fifth Avenue
Suite 3308
New York
N.Y. 10118

360 York Road, RR 4
Niagara-on-the-Lake
Ontario, Canada
L0S 1J0

73 Lime Walk
Headington
Oxford OX3 7AD
United Kingdom

Cataloging in Publication Data
Kalman, Bobbie, 1947-
  Bugs and other insects

(Crabapples)
Includes index.

ISBN 0-86505-613-7 (library bound)   ISBN 0-86505-713-3 (pbk.)
This book looks at the bodies and habits of insects, as well as different members of the insect family.

1. Insects - Juvenile literature. I. Everts, Tammy, 1970-
II. Title. III. Series: Kalman, Bobbie, 1947-   . Crabapples.

QL467.2.K35 1994   j595.7   LC 94-22904
                                                      CIP

What is in this book?

What is an insect?

Some insects are big. Some are small. Some have wings. Some do not. Some people call all insects "bugs," but bugs are just one kind of insect. Insects have three body parts—a head, thorax, and abdomen.

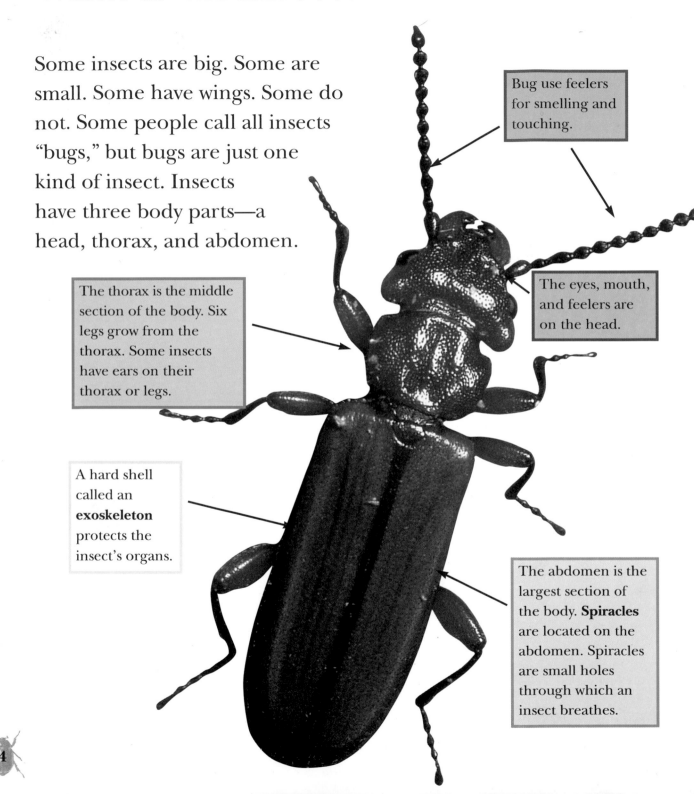

Bug use feelers for smelling and touching.

The eyes, mouth, and feelers are on the head.

The thorax is the middle section of the body. Six legs grow from the thorax. Some insects have ears on their thorax or legs.

A hard shell called an **exoskeleton** protects the insect's organs.

The abdomen is the largest section of the body. **Spiracles** are located on the abdomen. Spiracles are small holes through which an insect breathes.

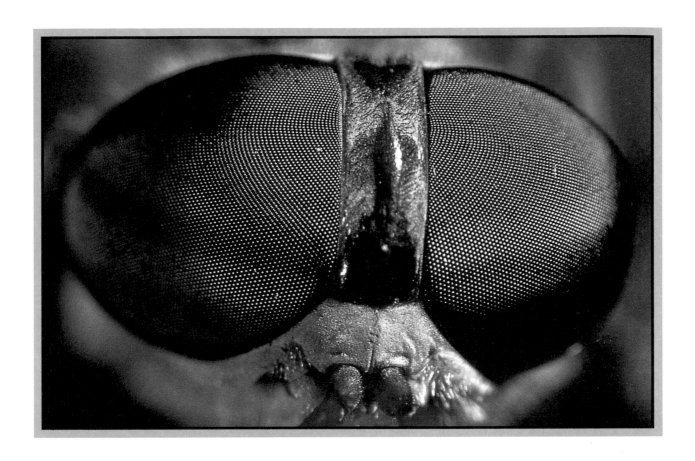

Insects have large **compound eyes**. Compound eyes have many tiny parts called **facets**. Simple eyes have only one facet. Humans have simple eyes.

Insects see differently than we do. Each facet in their eyes works separately. The insect sees hundreds, or even thousands, of pictures of the same thing. It can sense when something is moving above, in front, beside, or behind its body.

facet

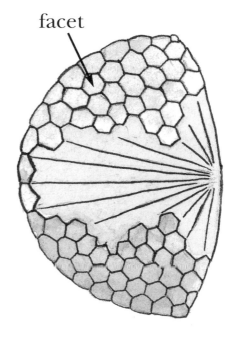

Growing and changing

1 A female insect lays an egg or a bunch of eggs. These eggs are covered by an **egg case**. The egg case protects the eggs and holds them together.

Insects come from eggs. They grow into adults in a series of steps called **metamorphosis**. Metamorphosis means change.

There are two types of metamorphosis: incomplete and complete. **Incomplete metamorphosis** has three stages: egg, nymph, and adult. Crickets and bugs go through incomplete metamorphosis.

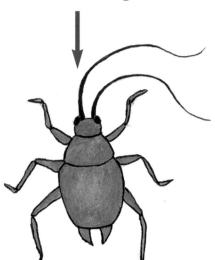

2 An insect hatches from an egg. It is called a **nymph** and looks like a small adult insect. The nymph sheds, or **molts**, its skin several times as it grows.

3 The insect stops molting when it reaches adult size. Some insects have grown wings by this stage.

Some insects, such as butterflies and moths, go through **complete metamorphosis**. Complete metamorphosis has four stages: egg, larva, pupa, and adult.

1 The female insect lays an egg or a bunch of eggs.

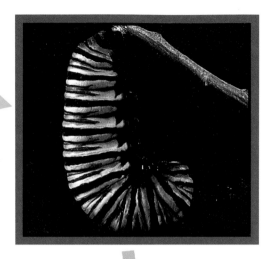

2 The **larva** breaks out of the egg. The larva molts its skin several times.

4 Inside the chrysalis, the larva changes into an adult. The adult then breaks out of the chrysalis.

3 In the **pupa** stage, the larva makes a **cocoon** around itself. A butterfly cocoon is called a **chrysalis**.

Clever disguises

Insects have colors and patterns that help them hide. This clever cover-up is called **camouflage**.

Some insects are the same color as the place where they live. The grizzled mantis blends in with the moss on which it rests. Do you see it?

Some caterpillars, moths, and butterflies have large spots that look like eyes. These spots are called **eyespots**. Eyespots frighten away enemies.

Some insects, such as this velvet ant, have beautiful bright colors. Bright colors give warnings, such as "Watch out! I taste awful," or "Stay away! I am poisonous." An animal that has eaten a colorful insect will probably not eat one again!

Bug talk

Insects buzz, chirp, whine, and sing. Some insect sounds have a message, such as "I am looking for a mate," or "Keep out of my territory!" The next time you are outdoors, listen to the sounds of insects and try to guess their message!

cricket

The cricket rubs its wings together to make a happy, chirping song. The katydid above is a grasshopper that makes many loud calls. One of its chirps seems to say the words "Katy did, Katy did!"

Grasshoppers have a row of bumps on each back leg. They rub their back leg against a wing to make a chirping sound. Run your fingernail over the teeth of a comb to make a similar sound.

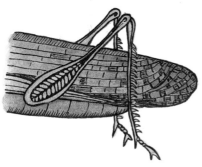

Insect food

Each insect likes certain foods. Some eat the leaves of plants. Some eat dead animals. Some eat garbage. Some eat wood. Some even drink blood! The acorn weevil below makes a hole in an acorn to eat the tasty nut inside.

Many insects hunt other insects for food. The praying mantis below is a good hunter. It eats smaller insects such as crickets. It can grab an insect with its strong front legs and hold on tight as it munches.

Insects are an important part of nature. Some clean up the earth by eating dead plants and animals. The predacious diving beetle in the picture above is eating a dead frog.

The insect family tree

There are over one million species of insects that are known by people! Scientists believe that there may be two or three million more types of insects that have not yet been discovered!

There are many branches on the insect family tree. The most common insect groups are bugs, beetles, bees and wasps, butterflies and moths, flies, grasshoppers and crickets, ants, and termites. There are many other kinds of insects but too many to name.

termites

grasshoppers and crickets

flies

ants

beetles

butterflies
and moths

bees and
wasps

bugs

Make your own "insect tree"
and add your favorite insects!

15

The real bugs

Bugs come in all shapes, colors, and sizes. Some bugs, such as the koa bug on the opposite page, are very beautiful.

Although bugs are different from one another, they have one thing in common. They all eat liquid food through a **rostrum**. The rostrum is a long tube that is like a drinking straw. This assassin bug spits poisonous saliva through its rostrum.

rostrum

Beetles

stag beetle

There are more beetles than any other kind of insect. Beetles live in deserts, caves, beaches, forests, and fields. Some live in rivers, streams, and lakes. Most beetles eat plants, but some eat other insects or dead animals. The colorful snout beetles below have a special mouth for eating plants.

18

A beetle's front wings are hard cases called **elytra**. Underneath are another pair of wings. The elytra protect these delicate wings when the beetle is not flying.

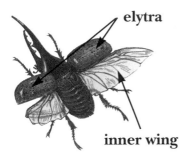

elytra

inner wing

Look at the rhinoceros beetle below. All beetles have an extra-hard exoskeleton. That is why many people call beetles "armored insects."

Bee or wasp?

Bees and wasps are the same in many ways. Some live in large groups called **colonies** or **hives**. Bee colonies are often found in hollow trees. Most wasps build nests of mud or chewed-up wood.

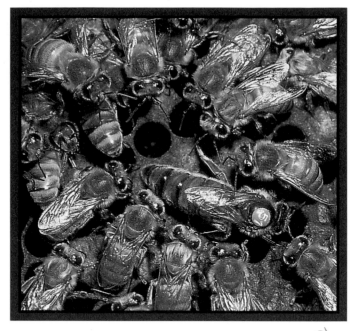

The **queen** is the biggest insect in the colony. She lays all the eggs. There are only a few **drones**, or males, in a colony. They mate with the queen and then die. Most of the bees and wasps in a colony are females called **workers**. They build the nest and collect food.

Bees and wasps are different in some ways. Bees have fat, fuzzy bodies. Wasps have thin bodies without any fuzz. Both bees and wasps have a stinger. A wasp can use its stinger many times. A bee stings once, and then it dies.

Worker bees collect a syrup called **nectar** from flowers. As they fly from flower to flower, **pollen** sticks to their body. Pollen is a yellow dust found on flowers. Some of the pollen rubs off on the next flower. Flowers use pollen from other flowers to make seeds.

Butterflies and moths

Butterflies and moths are alike in several ways. Both are caterpillars when they are young. Adult butterflies and moths drink nectar from flowers. Their wings are covered with tiny scales that come off easily if you touch them. The scales look like dust on your fingers.

Most adult butterflies and moths die when the weather gets cold, but some, such as the monarch butterfly, fly to warmer places. They leave in the fall and return in the spring. This long trip is called **migration**.

Butterflies and moths come in many sizes and colors. Read the features beside each photograph. Can you tell which is the moth and which is the butterfly?

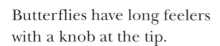

Butterflies have long feelers with a knob at the tip.

Butterflies bring their wings up over their bodies when they rest.

Butterflies are usually large and colorful.

Most butterflies fly during the day.

Moth feelers come in many shapes and sizes.

Moths fold their wings close to their body or spread them sideways when they rest.

Moths are usually smaller and less colorful than butterflies.

Most moths fly at night.

Flies

dragonfly

Flying insects are often called flies, but some are not real flies. The common housefly is the best-known fly. The mosquito below and the green bot fly on the opposite page are flies. The dragonfly, however, is not a fly.

True flies have only two wings. They can
fly quickly and hover in the air. Some
can even fly backwards! Flies have special
feet that allow them to walk on ceilings.

Flies can be found almost everywhere.
They eat almost anything. Many flies
land on people, animals, and food. They
can spread diseases by carrying germs.

common house fly

Crickets and grasshoppers

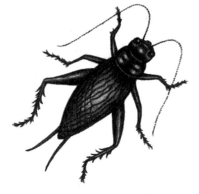

Crickets and grasshoppers live almost anywhere, but they prefer warm places. Tree crickets, such as the one below, live in trees. They are most active at night.

Grasshoppers have wings for flying.
They have long, strong legs for leaping.
Sometimes a grasshopper loses a leg
when a hungry bird grabs it in its beak.
A new leg then grows to replace the
leg that was lost.

Ants

Ants can be yellow, brown, red, or black. They live all over the world, but they are most common in warm places. Ants eat almost anything from seeds to dead animals.

Ants are very strong. They can lift things that are much bigger than they are. A group of ants can carry a dead mouse!

Termites

Termites are sometimes called white ants, but they are not ants. Some termites eat wood. When these termites make their homes in telephone poles or houses, they cause a lot of damage.

Some types of termites build **termitaries** from earth. Inside each huge mound is a maze of rooms and tunnels. Some of the tunnels reach far down into the ground. These deep tunnels are water wells.

Is this an insect?

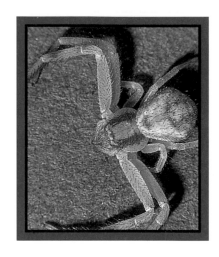

Do you remember what an insect is? An insect is small. It has six legs and three body parts—a head, thorax, and abdomen. It has feelers on its head. Some creatures look like insects, but they are not insects.

Spiders have eight legs. They have two body parts—a head and an abdomen. Are spiders insects?

The centipede has a long body like that of a caterpillar. It has feelers and dozens of legs. It has many body parts. Is the centipede an insect?

Worms have long, slender bodies. They do not have feelers. Worms have many body parts, but most do not have legs. Are worms insects?

If you guess that none of these creatures is an insect, you are right!

Words to know

camouflage Patterns or colors that help an animal hide

chrysalis A butterfly cocoon

colony A group of insects

drone A male bee or wasp

elytra The hard pair of wings that protects the inner wings of a beetle

metamorphosis The growing and changing from egg to adult

migrate To move a long distance

organ A part of the body that is necessary to live

pollen A fine yellow powder that is found in flowers

rostrum The tubelike mouthpart of a bug

spiracle A small hole through which an insect breathes

Index

What is in the picture?

Here is more information about the photographs in this book.

page:

front cover	The koa bug lives in Hawaii.
back cover	A kind of weevil
title page	This *neptunides stanleyi* lives in Africa.
4	A red flat bark beetle
5	This closeup shows the eyes of a horsefly.
7	These pictures show steps in the metamorphosis of a monarch butterfly.
8	A six-spotted green tiger beetle
9 (top)	This grizzled mantis was photographed in Florida.
9 (middle)	A tiger swallowtail butterfly larva
9 (bottom)	The velvet ant is more closely related to wasps than to ants.
10	Katydids live throughout North America.
11	Each kind of grasshopper has a unique song.
12	The acorn weevil has a special mouth that allows it to "drill" into hard nut shells.
13 (left)	Sometimes female praying mantises eat male mantises!
13 (right)	The word "predacious" means to catch and eat prey.
16	The bright colors of the koa bug warn enemies to stay away.
17	Different kinds of assassin bugs live all over the world.
18	There are more than 40,000 different kinds of snout beetles.

page:

19 (left)	Long-horned beetles are named for their long antennae.
19 (right)	The snout of a rhinoceros beetle resembles the horn of a rhinoceros.
20 (top)	The queen bee (with "51" on its back) sits in the midst of worker honeybees.
20 (bottom)	A wasp nest
21 (top)	Wasps can be found all over the world.
21 (bottom)	This bee has clumps of pollen attached to its legs.
23 (top)	A red admiral butterfly
23 (bottom)	The polyphemus moth lives all over North America.
24	This mosquito's belly is full of human blood.
25	Bot flies torment farm animals by laying eggs in their bodies.
26	Tree crickets chirp faster as the temperature outside gets warmer.
27	Grasshoppers use their wings to help them jump farther.
28	Leaf-cutter ants live in the rain forests of Central America.
29 (top)	This is a wood-dwelling termite.
29 (bottom)	This termite mound is in Africa.
30 (top)	A minute crab spider
30 (middle)	Centipedes use their venom to stun insects that they hunt.
30 (bottom)	Earthworms eat soil to get nourishment.

2 3 4 5 6 7 8 9 0 Printed in USA 3 2 1 0 9 8 7 6 5